WORDS OF A MAGPIE

WORDS OF A MAGPIE

Written & Illustrated by
Annie Rich Thompson

WALNUT STREET
—PUBLISHING—

ISBN 979-8-9893320-8-3

Walnut Street Publishing
1645 S Holtzclaw Ave
Chattanooga, TN 37404

For my Grandmothers
Who gently taught me
To find myself

Table of Contents:

You may call me a magpie
I'm just glad I have so many stories
To sing about

Even though some of them are sad

"Mama, What's a Magpie?"

Part I:

Walking with Wildflowers

If I were a flower
I think I'd be a dandelion
Yes.
I would be tall
But small
With my face to the morning sun
When the sun gets too bright
I would close my petals up
To protect myself

I would have little seeds that blow
Like love notes through the breeze
And hopefully float somewhere
Where someone needs
The smile of a dandelion

Some people might call me a weed
But I know that I'm a flower
And I don't need them to know it

I wouldn't mind living next to a tree
Or a smooth stone
Befriend bees
And wave and dance in the wind

I wouldn't mind it... no.
I think I wouldn't mind it.
I think if I was a flower
I'd be a dandelion

"In Another Life, I'm a Dandelion"

When I think I'm no-one's
cup of tea
I think of dandelions
The way mankind has vilified
The little yellow flowers

I think how wonderful their leaves
Taste on a summer salad
How beautiful the yellow is
When the flowers dye my fabric

We work so hard to hate the weed
The dandelion flower
Yet so many wishes rely upon
It's tiny, fuzzy power

So if you feel unwanted
Call upon the dandelions
Despite the way they're chased away
They always come back stronger

Call me Dandelion, Darling
For dandelion wine is sweet
I'll let them teach me how to dance
In the spring and summer breeze

Dandelions stand their ground
Even if they are not wanted
I make myself a flower crown
And be the Dandelion Queen

"Lady of the Dandelions"

Oh, to wander
Until I am lost
Among the daffodils

Like the moth
I will grow
Maybe this dark season
Is just a cocoon

I never see insects worry
They know their job
They do it
Ants often look concerned
When they lose their way,
I suppose.
I understand ants.

Being myself feels raw
And naked these days
It will take work
To peel back these costumes
I've made
Which one is me?
While I ponder

6

I think I will wander
Among the daffodils

"Cocoon"

Is it rain
Or a watering can
Reminding you
To take care of yourself

Why do we get sad when it rains
It's the garden's
Favorite part
Of the day

"Self Care for a Flower"

I'm just a flower
Growing in rocky soil

With a little water and sunshine
I'll turn out alright

Don't compare yourself to the ones
Growing in a garden

"It's Okay to Grow Here"

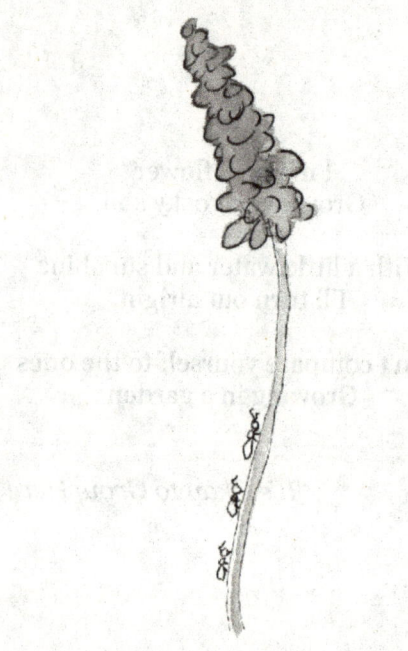

Do wildflowers sleep
When the moon comes out?

Do they sit quietly all day
And accept that they are called weeds

At night, do they dance
In the moonlight

Like the flowers
They are

"The Dance of the Wildflowers"

We water each other's gardens
And sometimes brambles climb
But she gently untangles
all my flowers
And lets me take my thyme

Sometimes when I
can't find the light
She sings to me so I'll still grow
And sits and holds my wilting leaves
Together we gather seeds to sow

Sometimes I help her stand
I tie a stick to growing stems
And she always finds a way
To grow and thrive again

Stretching tall, we do know
We don't have to grow alone
We may be different flowers
But each have beauty of our own

"My Friends are Like Flowers"

I wonder if I'm the only human that
some flowers ever see.
Did they witness me dancing?
Or crying by the creek?
Do they think humans are joyful?
Or sorrowful and bleak...
Or maybe do they think I am resilient
at least?

Were they the flowers that I spoke to
On the trail when I went in
To the woods to find myself
Before I came back out again

Was it the only conversation
That they have ever had
Those little blooming flowers
That grew along my path

Are you the only human
That some flowers have ever seen?
Did you speak to them with kindness
Did you tell them anything?
The fleeting witnesses of summer
walks

I take through the dappled wood
I wonder if they heard my thoughts
I'd like to think they could

"Wildflower Witness"

I hope you find some peace
Between the pages of a book
And notice all the little things
And take the time to look

Like dandelions waving
And the smallest little bee
And moss that feels like carpet
Tiny mushrooms that you see

I hope you stop to wonder
And I hope you stop to breathe
The greatest magic that we have
Is waiting just within our reach

"Little Wonders"

I know I'm strong
But sometimes

I wish I didn't have to work so hard
To push through pavement

To bloom

"Parking Lot"

I wish I could turn memories upside
down
And hang them on a windowsill

The way I dry flowers
So I don't have to let them go

*"I don't want to forget
anything about you"*

Some people are flowers
You see
Not literally

But
My Grandmomma
Lives on in the African violets on my
window shelf
The Irises my cousin replanted in her
garden
The roses she taught me to prune
And the azaleas she loved so dearly

The really beautiful people
Don't just live
They bloom
And because of them
We bloom, too

"Margie"

Part II:

Under the Trees

The forest feels like home
With beds of leaves
For resting
Carpets of moss
For quiet walks
With bare feet

A roof of branches
Beckons me
To tuck away
From soft rain

The only thing I need
Is the bird songs
And the best conversation
Is the one I overhear
From them
And the squirrels

I think certainly
The forest feels like home
And we should go home
More often

"My Soul Lives Here"

I lay in the loam
As I pondered my flaws
I slept with the roots
With my skin on the moss

The wind above whispered
To love every inch
Of my bare human body
My freckles, my ribs

My spine like a fern
My doe-colored eyes
My curves like the rivers
My height like a pine

I lay and I listened
Near the cold forest spring
As the forest she whispered
"You lovely wild thing"

"My Bones Rest"

I go into the forest
With my grief in my heart
And let the trees lift it from me
At least in part

I pour it into flower cups
And lay it on the grass
And let the moss absorb it
As the time will slowly pass

The leaves quietly whisper
For me to feel my pain
And let it pour into the earth
Like water after rain

Don't carry more of it
than you must
When grief makes you unsteady
The trees have roots that
run so deep
To help you carry what is heavy

"My Therapist is a Tree"

Sometimes she wished
She could be just like them
With towering branches
And soft leaves and stems

They swayed in the storms
Danced in the rain
Their roots ran so deep
And anchored their pain

Their arms stretching far
And home to so many
Some flowering bright
Some stoic and heavy

She learned from the trees
To slow and to watch
To heal over time
Like scars on the bark

So she took what she learned
And watered her roots
Stood firm in the storms
And she started to bloom

"Watering My Own Roots"

I am overcome
When I think of the strength
Of Women

Like Willows
They grow
With outstretched arms
Sheltering those
Who seek refuge beneath their
branches

Like willows
The women
Require water
Love
And Sunlight
To grow

Like Willows
Each is rare
And storms may bend them
But rarely do they break

And when they do
Buds form

And still
They survive

Do you know the way that women
carry the world?
In wombs and hearts and minds?
Like willows
Rooting the soil and providing a
foundation for you to stand on
And a way to climb

She is a tall and beautiful relic
But the world so often treats her as a
weed
Who in your life is a willow
Or are you yourself a seed?

Grow, little willow
Like the ones who came before
I am overcome
when I think of the strength of
women
Like willows

"Willow Woman"

And slowly
I began to grow into myself
The way a tree gradually returns to
herself
After a long winter

"People Have Seasons, Too"

I wandered the forest
On paths of red leaves
As twilight was falling
And talked to the trees

I stopped at the biggest
And oldest that stood
To ask them advice
As a young woman should

I arrived in a clearing
Where the cherry tree stretched
Up towards the dim sky
And I sat down and wept

She listened in quiet
As rain fell to earth
Her broken branches proof
She understands hurt

As the small raindrops fell
And night embraced day
the towering trees
Took some pain away

"Cherry Tree Funeral"

Do the trees grow jealous
as we run past
That they are still
And we are not

Or do they smile
As they know having deep roots
And stillness
Is good for the soul

Do they laugh
With gentle rustles of leaves
As we hurry past

Do they stretch out their limbs,
growing strong and tall
To show us
That being planted
And growing through rock
Makes them strong

I smile at the trees as I run past
Wondering
Do they wish they could run too

Or should I try
To be more like the trees

"What the Trees Teach Us"

They said when I grew up
I'd stop running through woods
I'd put on my shoes
And I'd stop reading books

"You just won't have time"
"You'll see what its like"
But today I went walking
In bare feet for a time

I listened to the wind
As it rustles the leaves
And I sat on a log
And talked to the trees

I read from a book
About imaginary things
And I let down my hair
As the little birds sing

My heart's much more heavy
Than when I was small
But their words never silenced
The forest's sweet call

If I didn't still run
Through the woods and the creeks
I think I'd have broken
From all that I've seen

But I go into the wild
With bare feet and book
And the forest returns something
The world though that it took

"Sanctuary"

I watched each morning
As the trees
Slowly
Stepped out of their sunset gowns
The colors of fire - red and yellow
Letting them slip to the ground
Until they were bare

Reaching towards the sky
With naked branches
For the early autumn light
As it stretches from the mountain
ridge
And kisses the tallest tree tops first
Warming the fall and winter trunks
With golden rays

Only the mountain sunrise
Shimmers like that

Don't worry for the trees
As they stand undressed
They know each winter season
They must let old things go

Their roots run deep
Letting them Rest
And ready
For the time when they will grow

"Sunset Gowns"

Everything
I ever loved
Leaves footprints on my heart

Like rabbit prints
Under slumbering trees
In the fresh fallen snow

"Missouri Snow"

I didn't think about how
The Mountains are in my blood

Does my body know, do you think?
Is that why it feels like coming home?

"I'm Home Again"

High above the oceans
Peaks rise from valleys green
In the west there is a citadel
Grown of rock and clothed in trees

Should your soul grow tired or weary
Or the broken need respite
Drive deep into the mountains
Where the rivers run with light

Where the fish swim cold
And beavers live
And moose and mule deer climb
Come lay your head
On hallowed ground
And sleep beneath starlight

Fish for your meals
Walk long and far
And look out across the meadows
Allow the streams and rivers there
To wash and heal your spirit

"The Valley that Raised Me"

Part III:

Crossing the Stream

Each visit to a mountain creek
Washes darkness away easily
It makes sense
The water raised me

Tennessee cold water
Over tiny toes
As I played in the streams
Near my first home

Each place I've lived since
I found the water
I feel I must be
The river's daughter

"River's Daughter"

Rivers run in curves around me
Lines around my back and body
I have curves
Like rivers
And like them
I am powerful

"Like Rivers"

I return to rivers

In every chapter of life
Somehow I find them
They find me
Flowing

They pull me back to myself
Every time

"Keep moving"
She says
"Keep flowing"
She says

"Cut your path out of the rock"
She says

Every Chapter
There was water
Waiting for me
Pulling me back
Into myself

"Find Me by the Water"

44

I've never been good at stepping
gently into things
Testing the water

I have always jumped in, run across,
spraying droplets everywhere
Some people don't like to be splashed

But many have seen my joy, and come
to join me

"Don' Forget to Jump In"

In a storm a stream grows stronger
Rushing over river banks
I understand the overflowing
There's only so much she can take

Some days my feelings spill all over
Flooding through my pens and paints
But in a storm so does a river
Filled with too much when it rains

"Overflowing"

"You will find a way"
I read it somewhere
Maybe on a bus stop post scribbled in
faded sharpie
Or on some page folded in the
internet
I smiled, I will find a way

I thought for so long finding my way
meant running through obstacles,
leaping over adversity
If I just keep going if I just fight hard
enough, I'll get there
I'll get there
I'll get there

I didn't realize that maybe
Finding my way
Involves slowing
Sitting by the stream
Laying by the log
Before slowly creeping over it

You don't catch the cold morning air
by grasping at it

You catch it
By breathing it in

Maybe the way I'm meant to find
Is found after much quiet reflection
Slowing and learning
Growth like an old oak
Rather than a clambering weed
Reaching for light with eager leaves

I am finding my way
Now that I have stopped to read the
trail signs
Now that I have stopped to listen
To the way the river runs
I thought I had to run like the river
But even she is steady

I am finding my way
Now that I have slowed
To find it

"River Reflections"

Part IV:

Into to the Ocean

Do you think God crafted us from the
ocean?
Did they pour the water in our blood
from the sea?
If not, then why do I always hear it?
-The ocean, calling to me

"Salty Blood"

I counted the seasons
Of young adulthood
By the golds or greens
Of the marsh grass

"Island Girl"

Sand
Counts time
With tides
And hourglasses

Does it remember
The boys I kissed
By the dunes?

Does it remember
The pain it washed away
Time
And time again
As the waves beat the shore
I stood upon?

Does it remember
Or merely count
The times
With tides
And hourglasses

"Sandy Kisses"

I thought it was either or, back then
Intimidating
Or Beautiful

But sharks are both

"It's Ok to Be Both"

I came to the ocean
And asked her why it is
Life can be so unrelenting
Why it hurts sometimes to live

She says - "Do you not see the way I
crash
Onto beach, against the sky?
The storms that rage
The salty tears
I never cease to cry?

My daughter, you will have your
storms
Your raging and your death
But like the ocean water child
You will also come to rest

You cannot have the lovely ocean
Without the raging of the seas
So accept the storms and cycles
That will always have to be"

"The Ocean Taught Me"

We try to decide
How our lives will go
I wonder if the ocean laughs
That we think we know

She knows the rules
The law of tides
The push and pull
All life abides

Next time you fight
To control your way
Think of the sea
And what she would say

"Salty Advice"

And I really just dream of
being like her
Beautiful, beloved, and terrifying

"Let Me Be Like the Sea"

I can't be your emotional harbor
Too many of these ships turned into
house boats
Sinking beneath my waves
And dragging me down with them

But I can be a lighthouse
A passage through the storm
To see you through
As you carry us to smoother waters

Put up your sails
This is no place for giving up
Dropped canvas like ghosts
Let's pull them up together and sail
you out to sea

"Put Your Life Jacket on First"

What is forever?
The distance the ocean stretches from
sands
Farther than I can reach
The length of a river that one day
meets beach
The time a cloud floats
Longer than I can see
They eventually end
But I think what I mean is

Is it not forever
How long our love lasts
Because it's how long we know it
Before our lives pass

Just because something is not forever
Doesn't mean it wasn't to me
Like rings on our finger
Or rings of a tree

They may have forever
of varying lengths
But we have our forever
And forevers form links

And across our forevers
A story unfolds
A chain that's unbreakable
A chain strong and old

"Our Little Forever"

Part V:

To Listen to
Songs of a Magpie

I feel comforted
Just to have a pen and paper
In my hand

Sometimes I never write anything
down
Like the possibility
Is enough

The safe space
Within the four sides
Of the page in front of me

My voice - physically represented
By my pen
No question
That it exists

"My Soul Speaks on Paper"

It took me 28 years to learn the word
"no"
I was taught words when I was an
infant
But learned to use my voice much
later
Putting my needs first seemed like
betrayal

Silence is not a virtue
So why is that a saying?

Do they teach it to boys, too?

"Stop Apologizing"

63

Do other women feel it too
The wave of anger at a penny drop
Because it falls and breaks the cage
I've so carefully build around my rage

That builds in 18 cent shards
Growing to a knife slicing through my
heart
I ignore it like a splinter
Until the last stone is thrown
"You should smile. do you want kids?
You should spend more time at
home"

It's the niceties that cut the deepest
Dripping with patriarchal glaze
Comments about my choices hidden
behind smiles
And helpful prayers that I'll learn my
place

But you'll act surprised when I fight
back
Each expectation I break, a new
spidering crack

64

in the mirror you insist
I must reflect submission and
obedience
But I dance in the slivers as I shatter
the mold
For all the women who can't
Who feel it too
As I dance I smile - unless a man tells
me to

"When I Speak Up"

Starry eyes and sparkles
She was here and gone too soon
Still some say they missed the way
she lit up every room

They were often takers
She gave so much she emptied out
The world replaced her starry eyes
With dark moon dust and doubt

It's hard to forget someone who gave
us
So much to remember
I don't recall just when she died
Summer or cold December

All I know now is she is gone
And I am what remains
A woman grown who left behind
The girl with so much pain

I couldn't save her and survive
I had to let her go
She spread her stars too far and wide
She was too young to know

I still recall her,
Many do
Before the stars all died
So now I work to light these sparks
That I can keep inside

"Grow Up and Light a Fire"

I found myself pondering
What I would say
If my child becomes a girl
And faces the world one day

If it tries to quiet her
Or take her voice away
If it tells her to sit still
Here is what I would say

"You only have so long
For your light to burn on earth.
A hundred years at most
So decide what it is worth.

When they say to be quiet
Say they don't own your voice
When they say to be still
Say it isn't their choice

If they say what you'll wear
Say this isn't your body
When they laugh at your dreams
Keep pursuing your hobbies

My darling just listen
To the voice in your heart
Don't let darkness here on earth
Tear you apart

Just keep your light shining
And listen to your heart
Feel God in the forest
And do your small part

To be your true self
And owe no one a thing
Except kindness when needed
Without any strings

You get to just live
And be who you are
Without fixing the world
Or healing their scars

When they say to be quiet
Raise your chin and say no
I hope you're defiant
Even more as you grow

I won't nurture obedience
I won't teach you to lead
I just want you to live
Any way that you need

You only have a hundred
Of these years here on earth
I hope you come wild
From the moment of birth

"Come Wild"

One thing
I don't know how to prepare for
Is if I have a daughter
How do I teach her to be confident

And strong
And careful

And own her body and be unashamed
But know the evil of men
Without scaring her
To be wary of the world
But live life to the fullest

How do I tell her
Who she loves is her choice
As long as they respect her choices

How do I teach her
That being a woman
Is hard

But my favorite thing about myself

How do I teach her

When I am still unlearning
The lessons
Taught to me

"A Woman's Dichotomy"

I don't know
When I realized
They had put me in a box

Built it slowly
Like it was supposed to be there
Disguising it
So I thought
It was a natural part of life

Wallpapered with constraint
Carpeted with fine floors to keep the
sound in
"You are safe if you stay in the box"
"We are safe if you stay in the box"

Now, I dismantle it a little each day
A bolt here
A nail there
Some days, I rest
Other days I shatter a window
Or kick down a board

I filled it with flowers
And painted murals on the walls

But even the most lovely of cages
Is still a cage

And now I know
They put us in a box

"Flower Boxes"

"Nobody Cares"
Are my favorite words these days
Say them to myself and remember all
the ways
I was told that God was watching -
and the boys - and my elders
Smile, be nice, and don't you dare
expose those shoulders

"The boys will stumble if you wear
your shorts above your knees"
If that's all it takes for men to fall, I
hope they do and break their teeth

"Be a good example, get good grades
and don't mess up"
It's up to me, a Christian, to fill
everybody's cup

If I can be the perfect sister
If I can be the tape and glue
Oh God everybody's watching
What would Jesus do?

Now I know none of it was fair

Asking a child to haul the weight
Of churches, men and family
I'm glad it's not too late

To return to heal the girl I was
To scream and bare my shoulders
To get tattoos and run barefoot
Despite that I am older

No one cares. And that is freedom
I've come to love this well
Despite the way the world tells little
girls
To be perfect or go to hell

"Nobody Cares"

I have an announcement
I have built boundaries
Welcome to my world of walls
Don't think it's a sad thing

Some of these boundaries
Are built of beautiful ivy
Or wall flowers
I've been watering

Some of these boundaries
Still let the light in
Or are paper thin
They require a gold pen
For entry

Others are brick walls
Or winding halls
There's plenty cause
I'm done letting in the ones who take

And

I have an announcement

I have built boundaries
It took years to realize
The free entry through my gates
Was not appreciated
I learned too late

So now
I have an announcement to make
I have built boundaries

"Out to Lunch"

Let yourself out
Do not abide by the boundaries
others built for you
Laugh into adversity
Or run at it
Whatever your soul tells you to do

We are only human
The days pass quickly
And your true self deserves to be
heard
You don't need to belong
To live

The ones you're meant for will find
you
Even if you cross the lines drawn for
you by the ones who want to keep you
small
And if they don't
You are better off with yourself than
with those who don't understand who
you are at all

"Thirty One Years of Lessons"

I miss the days I was just afraid
Of monsters in the dark
But now I know I'm safe from ghosts
But not a broken heart

"The Real Monster Under my Bed"

You don't have to explain
Why you feel broken

It doesn't matter what size the pebble
was
That shattered the glass

Don't let anyone tell you you
shouldn't feel it
While you're picking up the pieces

"It's ok to feel it"

Joy is cheap
If you've never known grief

I'm so happy for those
Who don't know the value
Of effortless gladness

The kind of happiness that isn't
chased by shadows
Or the feeling that it's fleeting
Little birds that will fly away when
the darkness comes

So my joy is priceless
Nuggets of gold
Shimmering in the darkness
Letting light in
Breaking up the natural
Sorrows of life

My joy is not cheap
It is intentional
I have to remind myself to seek it
It doesn't fall in my lap any longer

If you see me laughing
When you think I should be grieving
Keep it to yourself
My laughter is precious
It doesn't come as easily
As it did when I was younger

So I trade joys with God
With the universe
Precious, shining joys
Joy isn't cheap
If you know grief

"Joy is Cheap"

I realized I hadn't written
In the span of several days
My muses often silenced
By the sadness that does weigh

I think most poets find
Strength in writing about sorrow
That poems and more words pour out
When life causes them to wallow

But grief it seems to grip me
Frozen solid like I'm stone
The words dry up, the hands won't
paint
The muses leave my bones

I know my heart would lighten
If I brought myself to make
Any kind of art
But the sun is blocked by ache

So now I write these words
To pour a little of the dark

Onto page with ink
So there's not so much in my heart

"Fragments"

Hello again, August
Last year you were the hardest I've
fought
To get myself up off the ground
You know, I really thought

Our friendship was done
A setting sun,
the cold of night
My will to fight
Leaving my body and my bones
An empty home
That for a while
Tried to carry a child

But you arrived
And they said with time
That I would heal
I'd be just fine

But August you didn't
Lessen my pain
As all your days passed
With summer rains
I felt betrayed

But now I know
That I had to hold
All that sorrow

Till it was spent
You saw me through
August, I know
It wasn't you

That made me feel
As though I'd drown
One year has passed
And now I've found

A peace, of sorts
I'm happy you're here
I've come so far
I've shed my tears

So August,
Let us start again
I'm learning beginnings
Start with ends

"August"

I flew to you like a moth
towards the sun
But you weren't the sun

You were just a broken street lamp

"You Weren't the Right Light for Me"

It's been twelve years since you
cracked my heart open

But now I see you helped me let the
light in

"I Should Have Left First"

Sometimes people disappoint us

It is important not to blame them
For failing to fill the mold
We made for them

They are not the key to fit the lock
Of our happiness

We have to unlock that door
For ourselves

"I'm Sorry I Locked You Out"

I've never been any good
At taking a step
Without a map of where my steps will
lead

What if the step into the unknown
Is over a cliff
Into shark infested waters

Or worst of all
What if the next step
Doesn't take me anywhere
At all

*"But What if It Takes You
Somewhere Beautiful"*

I didn't expect slowing down
To be such hard work
I thought that once I did
Things would be simpler

But slow
Is a skill

Identifying all of the golds the early
morning sun
Paints onto the greens of my
backyard
Takes time

Doing one thing
Is daring
Because you have to get to know it
Intimately
Not just the edges
And the parts
That are easy to define

"Maybe Tortoises Can Teach Me"

I couldn't find the sun
So I lit up every room

I pulled out lamps
And broken candles
To push the brightness through

The darkest corners all receded
And I turned the lights way up

Rejected every shadowed room
And sipped from empty cups

I didn't see the softness or the quiet of
the dark
That sometimes it's ok if your bright
light loses its spark

So I turned out every light
I let the candles flicker out
And wrapped in blankets in my bed
Telling the dark it was allowed

I let the darkness hold me
It gently told me I should feel

The grief that I'd been running from
So that I could heal

"Broken Candles"

My joy was once like little paper
butterflies
Thousands of them
Fluttering to land anywhere
Everywhere

I didn't know they were so fragile
Crumpling with each heartbreak
Each human mistake
That made them fall
Just bits of paper, now

I thought I couldn't get it back
But collected all the scraps
And put them in a pile
I didn't touch them for a while
But then

I took them out and taped them
Painted browns and greens and blues
And built some stronger paper moths
Out of tenacity and glue

My joy is rarer now
I try to still be soft

Though sometimes I dream of
butterflies
My moths, they are enough

"Pretty Paper Moths"

I'd like to take a moment
To grieve the words I didn't write
The paintings that I never made
That will never see the lights

Sometimes they never made it off my
head onto a page
Because I turned my insecurities into
a cage

Why don't I jump at each idea
And rush to write them down

Why do I sometimes convince myself
no-one would like it anyhow

Moving forward I want to cling to all
the words that fill my head
And let them out like little birds with
words and brush and pen

But I'd like to take a moment

To grieve the art I never made
I'll fight harder to let it out
Even if I am afraid

"Where Art Goes to Die"

Dear Reader:

My art is little pieces of me
Scattered into the world
Small gifts
Or just there because I needed
Not to hold them anymore

Pick one up
If you need it
Look at it
If you like

Some of them are darkness
And some are filled with light

"Little Pieces"

A Note from the Author:

I find inspiration in the small and the hidden - the first little wildflower messengers of spring, and the way the trees in the forest teach you when you sit still long enough. I hope you find the magic even in the hard times. I hope you write, or dance, or sing, or paint, even if you don't always feel confident. Even if life is dark. Your voice has meaning, and the world needs your art.

Special thanks to Walnut Street Publishing for encouraging my creative voice and providing a community for artists in the Chattanooga area.